THE LITTLE

WITCHLING of THE WOODS

A Magical Guide to Courage,
Calm & Confidence

Wilhelmina Woods

This Book

Belongs To

Book Cover by Tukotuku Publishing
Illustrations by Tukotuku Publishing
First edition 2025
Print ISBN:978-1-991410-69-6
Ebook ISBN:978-1-991410-70-2

For the Witchlings who
walk gently,
feel deeply,
and shine softly.
You are more
courageous than you
know,
and more magical
than you've ever
been told.

Welcome Dear Witchling,

If this book has found its way into your hands,
the Woods have already begun to open their lantern-lit paths to you.
You may not feel brave every day.
You may not feel calm every moment.
You may not always feel sure of your own light.
But that's why the forest called you here.
Inside these pages,
you will walk beneath whispering branches,
gather courage from glowing stones,
and learn the quiet magic that has been waiting
in your chest all along.
You don't need to know anything before you begin.
You don't need to be perfect,
or fearless,
or even ready.
You only need one thing:
A soft, curious heart.
Bring your feelings,
your questions,
your hopes,
and that small part of you that
wants to feel stronger
than the world sometimes lets you.
The Woods will take care of the rest.
Welcome, Witchling.
Your lantern is lit.
Your path is ready.

How to Use this Book

You don't have to read this quickly.

You don't have to feel brave every day.

You don't even have to start at Chapter One.

This book isn't a task — it's a forest.

Walk through it the way you would explore the woods:

• slowly, if you want

• quietly, if you need

• with curiosity, not urgency

Each chapter is a path.

Each ritual is a lantern.

You can follow them in order

or step into whichever one calls to you first.

Some days you may read many pages.

Some days you may only read one sentence

and let it glow in your chest for a while.

Both are magic.

If a ritual feels too big today,

come back to it tomorrow.

Or next week.

Or the day your heart feels ready.

There is no way to fail here.

This book is yours,

to wander, to rest inside,

to return to whenever the world feels loud.

The Woods are patient.

The magic is gentle.

Your light will carry you through.

Before You Enter the Woods

A Grounding Ritual for Witchlings

Before you step into the Witchling Woods,
take a moment to arrive,
not just with your body,
but with your breath.

Find Stillness

Sit or lie somewhere comfortable.
Feel where your body meets the earth,
the chair, the bed, the carpet.
Let your weight rest,
you don't have to hold yourself up alone.

Breathe Softly

Inhale slow like leaves lifting in a breeze.
Exhale like branches settling after wind.
Do this three times,
not perfectly, just gently.
Notice What's Here,

Look around and name:
3 things you can see
2 things you can feel
1 thing you can hear

You are arriving,

You are here.

Bring Your Hand to Your Heart
Feel for a beat,
a pulse, a thrum,
the small lantern living inside you.
Even if it's faint,
even if it flickers,
it is still light.

Whisper, Softly:

"My lantern is lit.
I am ready to walk gently."
When you feel even a small glow in your chest,
the forest door opens.
You may step inside now.

Chapter One

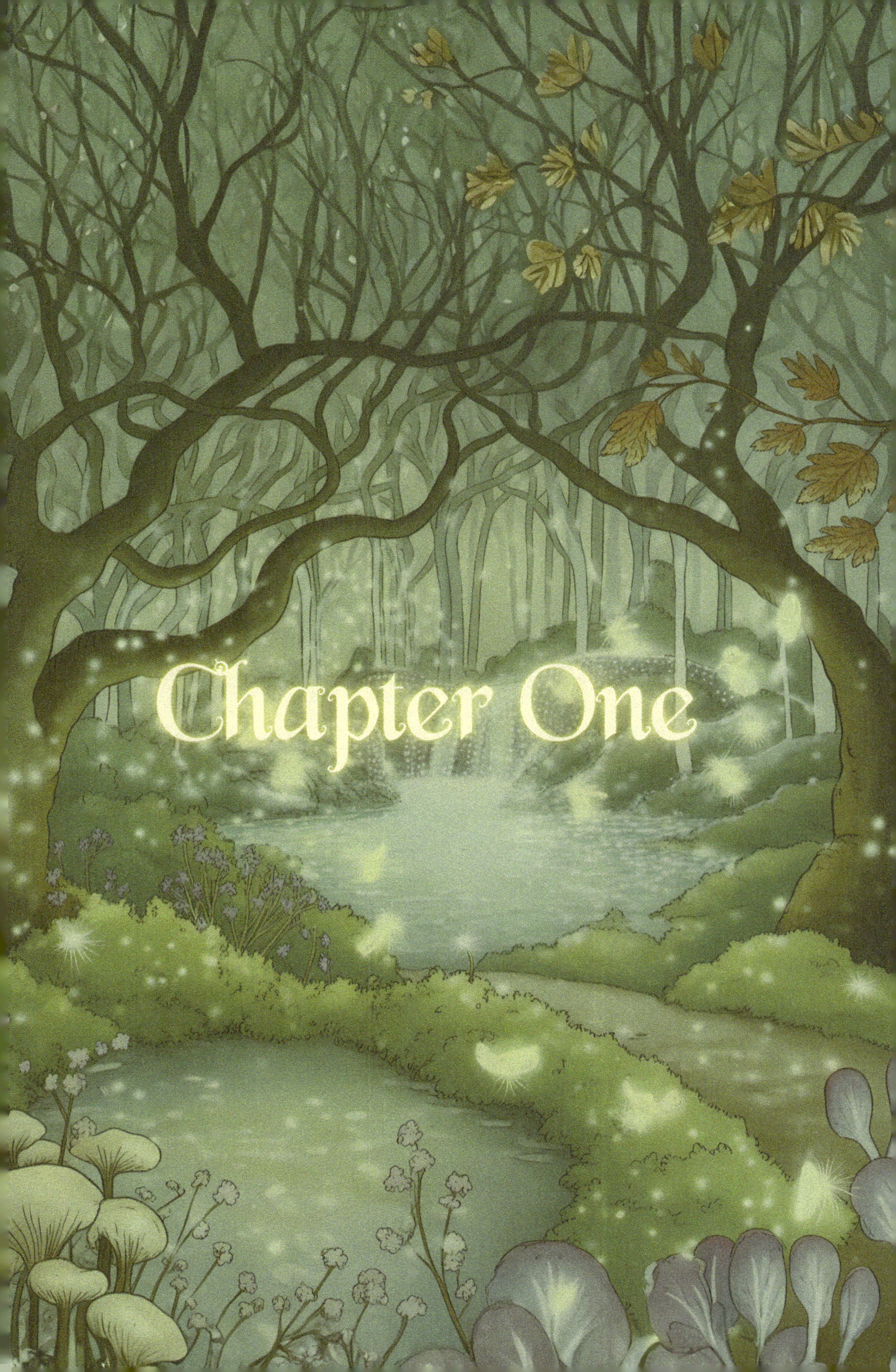

The Forest Door

In the quiet part of the evening, when the sky is the
color of cool ash and baby stars, you find it.
A doorway.
Not a wooden door or a stone one,
but a tall arch made of two ancient trees,
bowing toward each other as if sharing a secret.
Their branches twist together at the top, forming a shape
that feels like a welcome...

or an invitation.
The air here smells like rain and old magic —
the kind that doesn't try to impress you,
just hums softly beneath your skin,
as if it's always known your name.
A firefly drifts past your cheek, blinking once.

Then twice.
Then once more, as if saying:
"Are you ready?"
You step closer.
The moss under your boots is soft and springy.
The forest seems to breathe with you
slowly... gently...
as if matching your heartbeat.
Inside the archway, a faint warm glow flickers.

Like a lantern waiting.
Like it's been waiting all this time.
You don't know why,
but the glow doesn't feel like something
you're walking toward.
It feels like something that's walking with you.
You take one small step through the Forest Door.
And the moment you do,
the glow brightens.

Not because the forest sees you,
but because it knows you.
It knows the quiet courage you carry.
It knows the heavy feelings you've held alone.
It knows the questions you don't have words for yet.
And it knows the part of you —
the deep, soft, steady part —
that's ready for something new.

A warmth lifts inside your chest, gentle as a candle flame.
You don't realize until this moment that you've been holding
your breath.
Here, in this place,
the world doesn't feel too big.

It feels just big enough to hold you.
A small shape appears near your feet
a round stone glowing the color of dawn.
You kneel and touch it.
It hums.
A quiet, friendly hum.
A hum that says:
"You belong here."
And somewhere deep in the leaves above,
something shifts ,
a tail, a wing, a slow ripple of breath,
as if a great creature has opened one eye
and recognized you immediately.
You rise, holding the warm stone against your palm.
The forest watches.
And welcomes.
And waits.

You are no longer just a visitor.
You are a Witchling of the Woods now,
a keeper of calm,
a gatherer of courage,
a friend to the light inside you.
And the Forest Door closes softly behind you,
not to shut you in,
but to keep your doubts out.
Your journey begins with a single glow.
And it burns quietly in your hand.

A Witchling's First Step Spell

Stand or sit comfortably
with your hands resting softly by your sides.
Close your eyes.
Imagine an arch made of branches and leaves
woven together with soft lantern light.
Take one slow breath in.
Feel the air around you grow still,
like the Woods are listening.
Exhale gently.

Picture the Forest Door opening
just enough for you to see the glow inside.
Place one hand on your chest.
Feel your heartbeat,
steady, quiet, your own secret lantern.
Whisper softly:
"I step into the Woods with my light beside me."

Take one small step forward
(or imagine taking it).
This is your first step as a Witchling,
gentle and true.
Hold the moment for three breaths. The ritual is complete
when you feel even a small sense
of being supported from beneath.

Let the Woods welcome you
exactly as you are.

The ritual is complete
when you feel even the tiniest glow
in your chest.

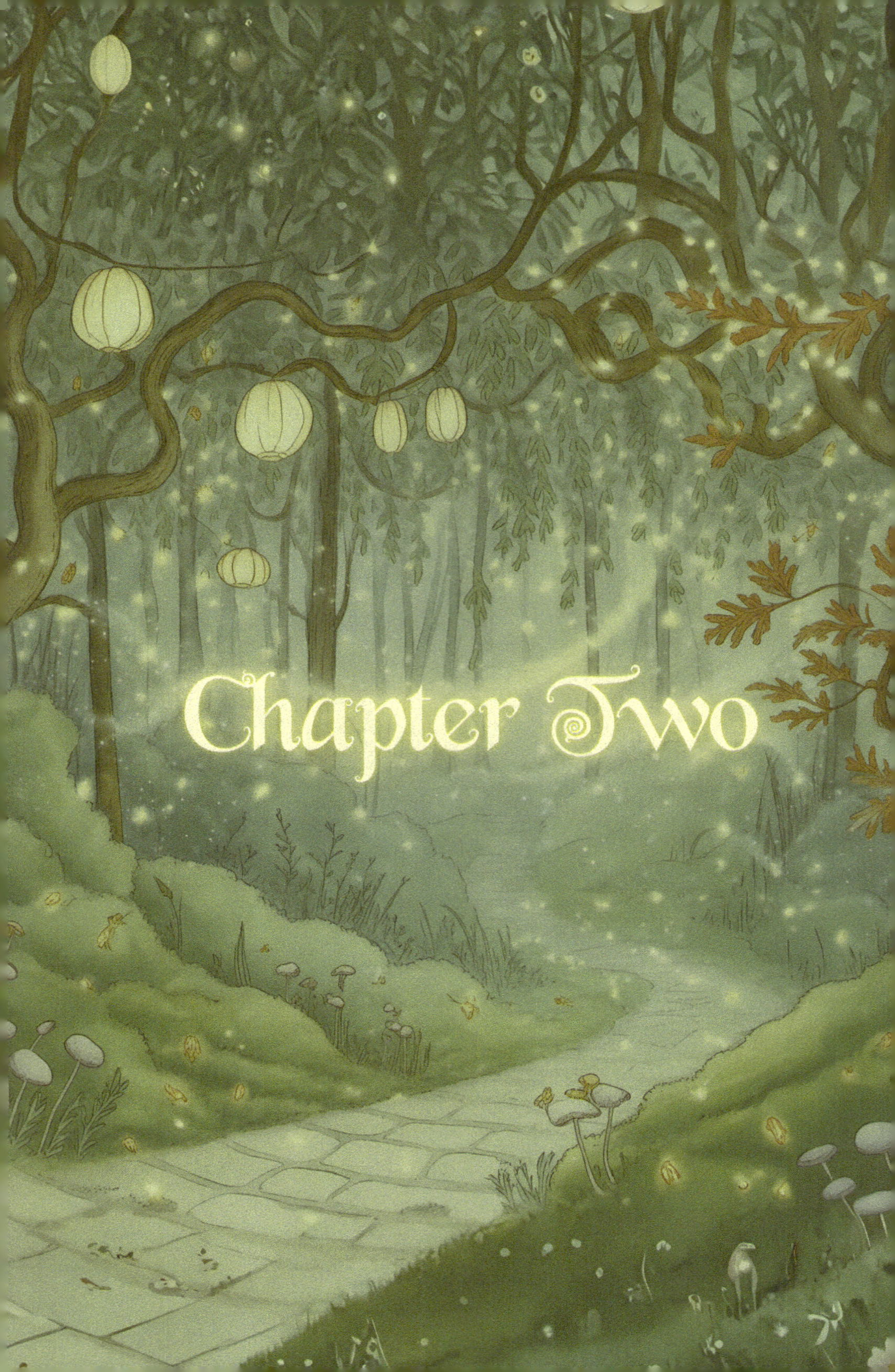

Chapter Two

The
Lantern Pathway

The glow in your hand warms a little more as you walk,
as if it's learning the rhythm of your heartbeat.
The forest around you is quiet,
but not silent.
It's the kind of quiet that feels alive,
the kind where every leaf has something gentle to say
if you listen long enough.
A small breeze drifts past your hood,
cool and patient, guiding you deeper into the woods.
Then you see it.

Not far ahead, hanging from the claw of a Guardian Dragon,
is a lantern.
Not just any lantern.
Your lantern.
The flame inside sways,
but doesn't flicker out.
It shines as if it has been waiting for this moment,
the moment you were brave enough to step through the Forest Door.
You reach for it.
And when your fingers brush the metal handle,
the light lifts, brightening just a little in greeting.

Warm.
Steady.
Certain.
The kind of light that says:
"I've been here all along.".

You lift the lantern,
and the glow from the Heartstone in your palm
seems to drift up into it,
as though the two lights know each other.
You notice something strange.
The lantern doesn't shine outward
like normal lanterns do.

It shines inward.
The light doesn't just illuminate the path.
It illuminates you,
the space around your chest,
the place where your courage lives,
the place where your truth whispers.
As you walk,
the lantern warms your hands,
your shoulders,
the inner place that gets cold when you're scared.

You feel it
a soft pulse inside the glow,
and suddenly you understand:
The lantern doesn't tell you where to go.
It simply reminds you
that you already know how to find your way.

A firefly drifts toward the lantern,
circling it once,
then settling on its rim like a tiny guardian.
And then another joins it.
And another.
Soon, a small cloud of fireflies travels with you,
their soft lights blinking like quiet encouragements.
With every step you take,
the forest seems to widen,
not to swallow you,
but to make room for you.
The lantern's glow reaches the path beneath your boots,
revealing patches of moss
and tiny mushrooms
that shine like stars fallen to the forest floor.

                              The pathway curves ahead,
                          twisting deeper into the Woods,
                                      as if asking:
                                  "Will you follow?"
                                  You step forward.
                                        One step.
                                     Then another.
                          Not because the path is easy,
                    but because the path feels meant for you
                              The lantern flickers once
                       in a way that almost feels like a nod.
                      And somewhere far above the treetops,
                          you hear a low, distant rumble.

Not threatening.
Not frightening.
Just... aware.
As if the guardian of this forest
has noticed your lantern has finally been lit.
You hold it a little closer to your heart.
And keep walking along the Lantern
Pathway,
its soft gold glow
carrying you forward
toward magic you haven't yet learned
and courage you didn't know you had.
toward magic you haven't yet learned

A Witchling's Light Stepping Spell

Sit or stand somewhere comfortable.
Let your shoulders soften
the way the Woods soften
when lanterns are lit.
Hold your hands together
as if cupping a small, warm light.
Close your eyes.
Imagine a winding forest path
lit by tiny lanterns hanging from branches
each one glowing just for you.

Take a slow breath in.
See the lanterns brighten.
Breathe out gently.
Watch their glow stretch further down the path.
Whisper softly:
"Each step I take brings me closer to my calm."

Imagine yourself taking one small step forward.
A lantern lights beneath your foot,
warm, safe, steady.
Take three more imagined steps.
With each one,
another lantern glows beneath you,
lighting the way
even if you can't see the whole path yet.
Rest your hands over your heart.
Feel the warmth settle inside you
like a lantern you carry everywhere.

The ritual is complete when you feel a little steadier than you did before.

Chapter Three

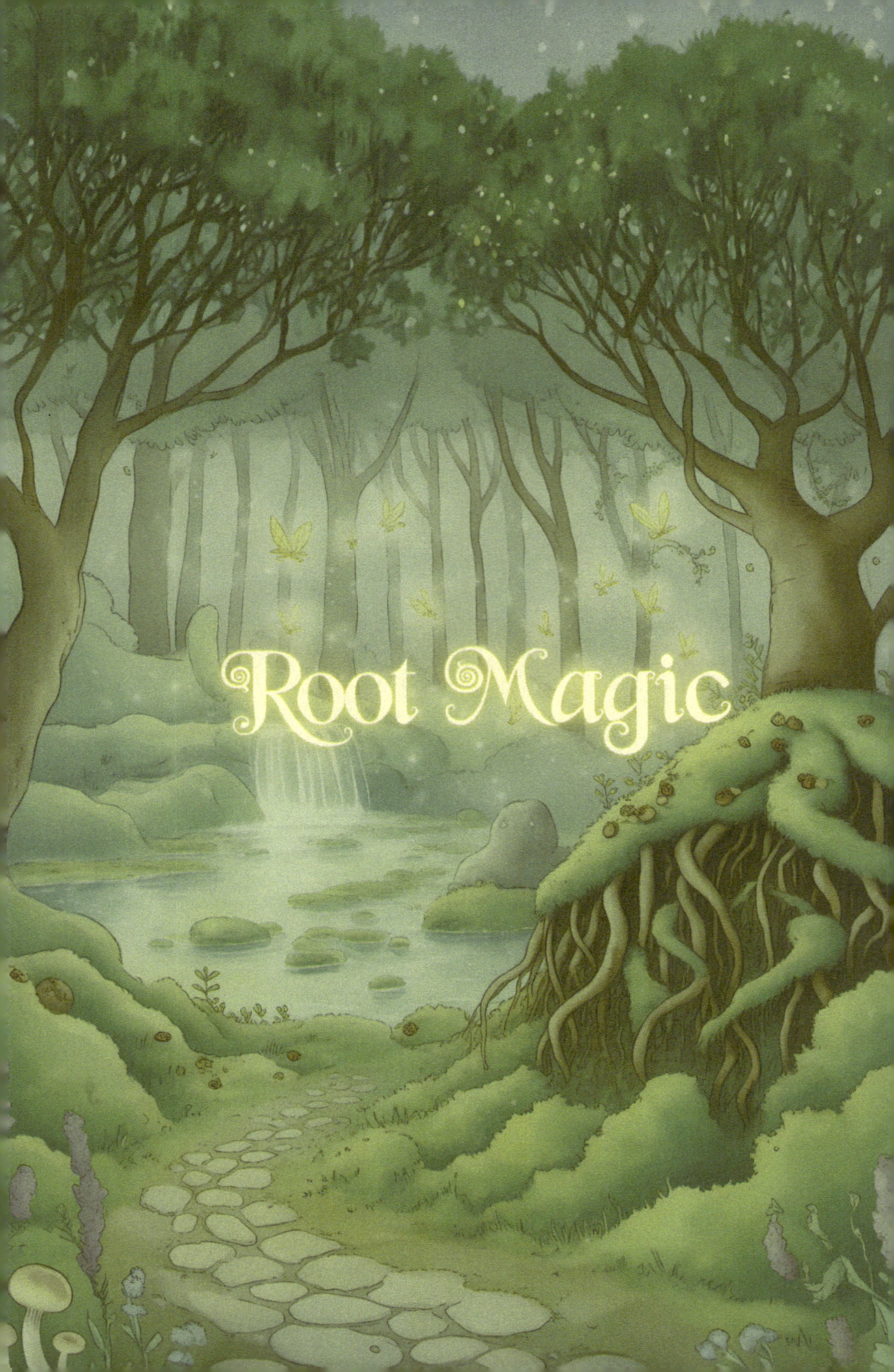
Root Magic

The Lantern Pathway leads you to a hill
that isn't really a hill at all,
it's a tangle of ancient roots,
as thick as your arms
and as old as forgotten stories.
They twist and weave together,
rising from the earth like a frozen wave,
each one covered in moss as soft
as midnight fur.
The moment you step onto them,
the forest quiets.
Not because it's empty,
but because it's listening.
The roots hum —
a low, steady, earth-deep sound
that feels like it's coming from
beneath everything:
beneath the stones,
beneath the soil,
beneath your own ribs.
You rest your hand against one of the
thickest roots.
And something shifts.
Not in the root —
in you.

A gentle warmth moves
up your arm,
into your chest,
like a slow exhale you didn't
realize you'd been holding back.
Root Magic doesn't flash or sparkle.
It doesn't roar like fire
or shimmer like moonlight.
It does something quieter.
Something deeper.
It reminds you
that you are held.

You sit on one of the largest roots,
its curve shaped perfectly for you
as if the forest carved it long ago
while waiting for this exact moment.
The lantern rests beside you,
its glow lighting the ridges of the tangled wood.
You curl your fingers into the moss.
It is cool,
and damp,
and alive.

And as you sit still,
you can feel the truth of this place:
The forest is not just around you.
The forest is with you.
You breathe in.
Deep.
Slow.
Easy.
And the roots seem to breathe with you.
A soft pulse rises from beneath the ground,
a rhythm older than language,
If steadier than fear,
stronger than worry.

It settles into your bones
like a promise:
"You are safe."
"You are supported."
"You are not alone."

Your feet press against the roots,
and the earth responds
not loudly,
but with a quiet certainty
that travels up your legs and into your chest.

The kind of certainty that says:
"You can stay here as long as you need."
A gentle rustle sweeps through the treetops above,
like a dragon sighing softly in its sleep —
a warm exhale that drifts down through branches
and settles warmly around your shoulders.
The roots beneath you glow for a moment,
faint and golden,
as if touched by the lantern's light.
Or maybe it's the other way around —
maybe the lantern remembers how to shine
because the roots remind it what strength feels like.
You close your eyes.
The ground holds you.
The air steadies you.
The forest waits with patient magic.
And in that quiet stillness,
Root Magic begins its work:
It brings you back to yourself.
Back to your breath.
Back to the place inside you
that cannot be shaken
even when the world feels too loud.

When you open your eyes again,
the forest hasn't changed.
But you have.
Somewhere inside you,
something that was trembling
is finally still.

You stand, lantern in hand.
The roots hum once more,
a final soft reminder:
Strength doesn't always roar.
Sometimes it grows slowly,
quietly,
deep beneath your feet.

And with the calm
of the earth settling into
your steps,
you continue along the path,
your light a little steadier now.

Sit or stand with your feet flat on the floor.
Let them rest the way roots rest—
soft, steady, quietly strong.
Close your eyes.
Imagine the earth beneath you
stretching deep and calm
like the ancient roots beneath the Woods.

Take a slow breath in.
As you inhale,
picture roots growing gently
from the soles of your feet
into the earth below.
Exhale softly.
Let the roots settle,
curling through soil,
soft and sure.
Place your hands on your thighs
or over your heart—
wherever feels safest.
Whisper quietly:
"I am rooted.
I am steady.
I am safe."

A Witchling's Grounding Spell

Breathe in again.
Imagine the earth sending warmth
up through your roots,
into your legs,
your chest,
your shoulders.
Breathe out.
Feel the weight of anything heavy
leaving your body
and sinking gently into the ground
where it can rest.

Stay for three breaths
in this grounded, rooted feeling—
strong but gentle,
held but free.

The ritual is complete
when you feel even a small sense
of being supported from beneath.

Chapter Four

Wind Spells

The Lantern Pathway curves alongside
a cluster of slender trees
whose silver bark glimmers as if kissed by moonlight.
Their branches sway
even though the air around you feels still.
A soft hush moves through the treetops
a whisper, not a gust,
as if the forest is breathing a secret into the sky.

You raise your lantern just a little.
That's when you notice it:
the air here feels different.
Alive.
Awake.
Listening.

A single leaf falls in a slow spiral,
twirling down as if carried by an invisible hand.
When it lands near your boots,
the air stirs again
a cool breath brushing your cheek.
And suddenly, you understand where you are.

The Grove of Wind Spells.
A place where the air learns your breath,
and your breath learns the air.
You take a small step forward.
The wind lifts your cloak gently,
almost in greeting.
Not pulling,
guiding.

                          You close your eyes.
              And the breeze moves around you
              the way a friend might step closer
                      to offer quiet company.
                          You breathe in.
                 The wind breathes with you.
                        You breathe out.

The wind follows,
soft, steady, certain.
It's not a storm-wind
or a rushing-wind
or the kind of wind that tangles your hair
and steals your hat.
This wind is gentle.
Patient.
Understanding.

A wind that knows
what it feels like
to carry too much.
A wind that wants to show you
how to let things go.
The air gathers in front of you,
lifting tiny sparkles of dust
that swirl in a lazy circle.
They drift upward, glowing gold
in the lantern light.
The wind is trying to teach you something.
So you listen.
And it becomes clear:
Wind Magic begins with a single breath
that feels like it belongs to you.
You breathe in again
slowly,
deeply,
letting the air fill the space in your chest
that sometimes feels tight
when the world becomes too heavy.

The wind hums softly,
 twining around your lantern's glow.
You breathe out,
soft, long,
like you are releasing something
you've been holding for far too long.

                              And the wind takes it.
                                    Not to erase it,
                                 not to dismiss it,
                        but to carry it for a little while
                                  so you don't have to.
                        A feather floats past your face.

It turns,
and turns again,
suspended by the slow spin of the air.
You breathe in.
The feather rises with your breath.
You breathe out.
It sinks gently,

                        landing without a sound.
                        And in that quiet moment
                     you learn the first Wind Spell:
                   When the air inside you feels tangled,
                    the air around you can help untie it.

Another breeze curls around your shoulders,
wrapping you in a soft, cool calm.
Somewhere deeper in the forest,
you hear a long, deep rumble,
the sound of wings shifting,
scales catching the light,
and a dragon exhaling
as if approving the spell you've just mastered.
You lift your lantern.
Its flame dances lightly —
not nervous,
but joyful.
Wind Magic has settled into your hands.
Into your steps.
Into your breath.
The forest breathes with you.
And for the first time in a long time,
you feel your breath belong to you.
You follow the breeze
as it guides you onward through the trees,
toward whatever magic waits next in the Woods.

A Witchling's Wind Spell of Calm

Stand still for a moment.
Feel your feet on the ground,
like roots resting gently beneath you.
Raise your hand to your chest.
Not to hold your heart tight,
but to remind it you're here.
Take one soft breath in.

Let the air fill your ribs,
like wind lifting the wings of a small bird.
Hold for a heartbeat.
Just long enough to feel the space
opening inside you.
Release slowly.
Imagine the wind carrying away
one small worry you no longer need to carry.
Repeat three times.

Each breath freeing a little more space,
each exhale untangling a little more air inside you.
Whisper this quietly:
"Wind, carry what I no longer need.
Leave me calm,
leave me clear,
leave me light."
Feel the breeze finish the spell.
Even if the air is still,
the wind inside you will move gently again.

The spell is complete when your breath feels like it fits you again.

Chapter Five

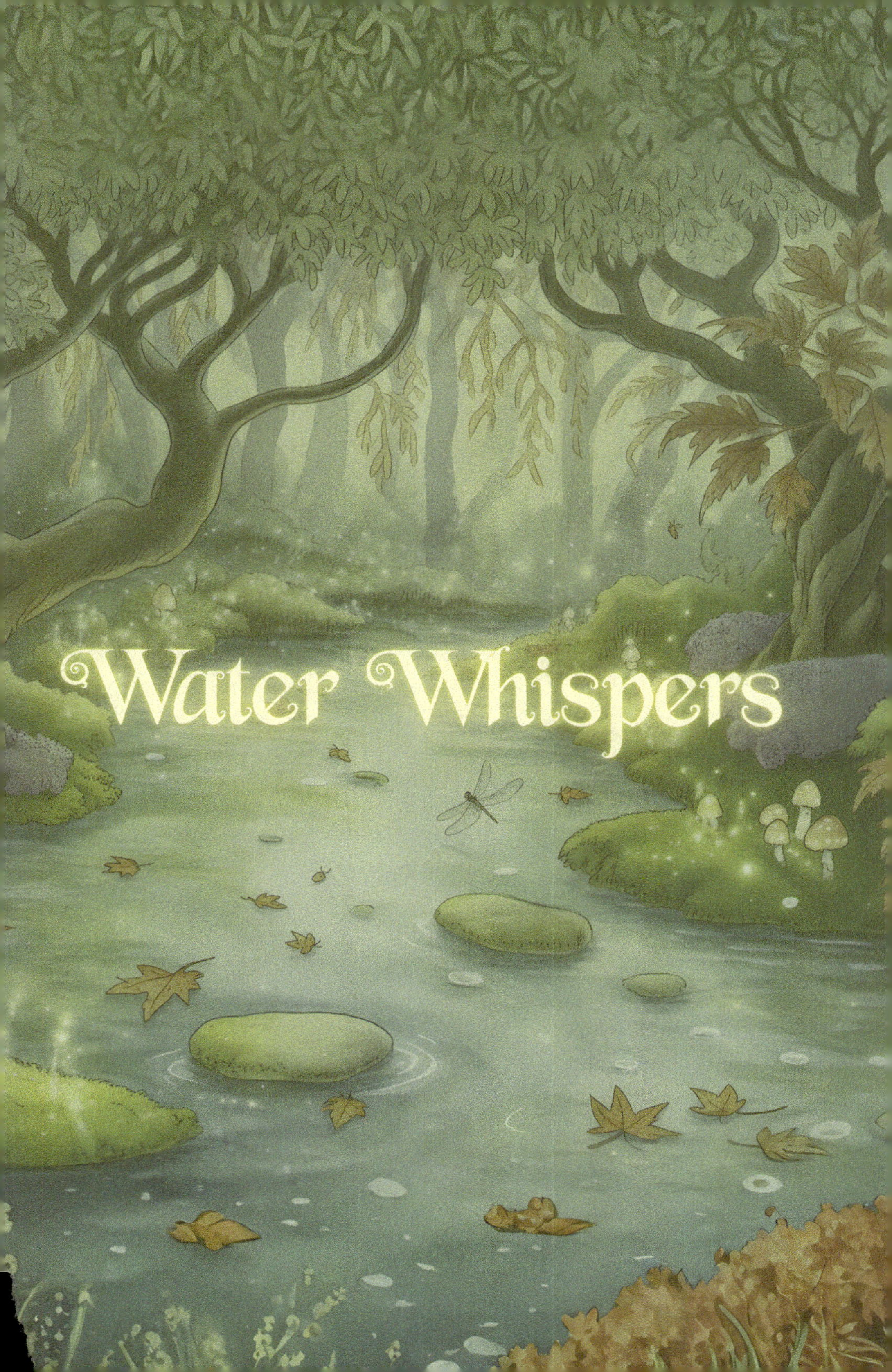
Water Whispers

The Lantern Pathway leads you to a place
where the forest grows softer,
quieter,
as if the trees themselves
are holding their breath.
You hear it before you see it
a gentle trickle,
a patient rhythm,
the sound of something moving
without rushing.
Then the path opens,
and you find the Whispering Creek.
A narrow stream winds through the clearing,
its waters dark as midnight glass
and bright as scattered stars.
Tiny ripples shimmer across its surface,
but the water isn't hurried.
It moves the way thoughts move
when you stop trying to control them
slow, curious,
free.

You kneel beside it.
The creek murmurs softly,
a voice made of silver threads and secrets.
You can't quite understand the words,
but you know the feeling:
This is a place
where feelings learn to flow again.
A small leaf lands on the surface of the water,
and instead of sinking
or fighting the current,
it drifts.
Effortless.
Unafraid.
Carried.
You watch it move,
and something inside you loosens,
a tightness you didn't even realize
you'd been holding.
The creek whispers to you
through the movement of its water:
"Nothing stays stuck forever."

A breeze brushes the side of your hood.
A dragonfly hovers above the stream,
its wings catching the light
in flashes of blue-green fire.
You dip your fingers into the water.
Cool.
Refreshing.
Alive.
The temperature startles you for a moment,
then settles into something comforting,
a reminder that some feelings
cool you down
when you need it most.
The creek shifts its current,
swirling around your wrist like a greeting.
You breathe out

And the water seems to breathe with you.
The Whispering Creek does not ask you
to explain your feelings.
It only asks you
to let them move.
Its presence settles you.
Not like something watching,
but like something witnessing.
The creek whispers again,
a gentle murmur that sounds almost like:
"Feel.
Then flow."
You close your eyes
and let your fingertips trail in the water,
as the creek carries away
the thoughts that feel too heavy
and brings back the ones
you forgot were yours.
When you stand,
your lantern glows brighter,
its light rippling softly
as if it, too, has learned
how to move more freely.

You follow the creek's bend
as it guides you back toward the forest path,
ready for whatever magic waits
just beyond the next clearing.
You trace small circles in the stream.
The ripples widen,
merge,
soften,
and disappear into the flow.
And you understand:
Water Magic doesn't want you
to push your emotions away
or hold them tight.
It simply wants you
to let them pass through you
like the current passing through the creek.
Somewhere high above the trees,
you hear a soft wingbeat,
a dragon shifting its great body
as if sensing a change in the air around you.

A Witchling's Water Whisper

Find your stillness.
Sit or stand with your lantern
(or your hands) resting gently
in your lap.
Imagine the Whispering Creek.
See the water moving
soft, steady, never rushing.
Touch two fingers to your other palm.
Let it feel like dipping your
hand into cool water.
Breathe in slowly.
Let your chest rise the way water lifts a leaf.
Breathe out softly.
Imagine one heavy feeling drifting downstream.

Repeat three times.
Each exhale letting go of something small.
Whisper quietly:
"Water, carry my heaviness.
Flow through me gently.
Leave me clear,
leave me soft,
leave me new."

The ritual is complete
when you feel something
inside you unclench.

Rest your hands on your heart or lantern.
Feel the calm settle like ripples becoming still.

Chapter Six

Circle Magic

The path turns left,
then right,
then narrows until the trees gather close
like old friends leaning in to whisper.
Your lantern glows brighter,
as though sensing the shift.
Up ahead, you see a ring of stones
smooth, pale, moss-kissed
placed in a perfect circle
in the middle of a clearing.
The air feels different here.
Not heavy.
Not sharp.
Just... clear.
You step toward the circle,
and the forest hushes
in a way that feels respectful,
like entering sacred space.
The stones hum softly
a low, steady tone,
the kind you feel in your ribs
before you hear it with your ears.

You stand at the edge of the circle.
The air around it is warm
but firm,
like the moment someone you trust
puts a gentle hand on your shoulder
and says:
"This is your space.
You are allowed to be here."
You lift your lantern.
Its glow stops exactly at the edge
of the stone ring,
as if recognizing the boundary.

A Circle of Protection.
Not the kind that keeps danger out.
The kind that keeps you in,
your thoughts, your feelings,
your sense of self.
You step inside.
The moment you do,
a hush falls across the clearing.
Not silence,
but presence.

The trees stand taller,
their branches arching overhead
like guardians.
The stones warm beneath your boots.
The air wraps around you
like a soft, invisible cloak,
fitting perfectly around your shape.
Inside the circle,
you feel:
Safe.
Centered.
Whole.
Here.

The lantern's flame brightens,
casting golden lines along the
inside of the stones.
You turn slowly,
feeling the boundary of the circle around you,
not a wall,
but a gentle reminder:
This is where you begin,
and the world ends.
Just for now.

You breathe.
Deep.
Slow.
Clear.
The circle amplifies your breath,
sending it out gently
through the trees
like a ribbon of quiet power.
You understand now:
Circle Magic isn't about pushing things away.
It's about inviting yourself in.
The wind stirs the leaves above
as something large shifts its weight
far above the treetops,
a dragon's attention settling on you
with warm approval.
You sense it,
not watching,
but witnessing
your growing strength.
You spread your fingers outward.
The circle responds,
a soft shimmer rising around you
like morning light touching dew.

Inside the circle,
you feel taller.
Not in your body,
but in your spirit.
You feel yourself.
And you realize:
Boundaries aren't shields.
They are shapes.
Your shape.
Claimed by you.

You lower your lantern.
The flame steadies,
burning bright and quiet.
The moment you step out of the circle,
you carry that steadiness with you,
around your heart,
around your mind,
around the tender places
that deserve gentle protection.
You follow the path onward,
the forest parting for you
like it recognizes a Witchling
who knows their own space.

A
Witchling's
Circle of Self

Stand or sit tall.
Imagine soft moss beneath you.
Spread your fingers outward.
Not to push away,
to define your space.
Take one slow breath in.
Feel your ribs widen
like a circle forming around you.
Exhale gently.
Let the circle settle.
Place your hand on your heart or lantern.
Feel its steady warmth.
Whisper softly:
"This is my space.
I protect it with kindness.
I fill it with truth.
I honor my shape."
Imagine a soft glow around your body,
pale gold,
breathable,
yours.
Hold the image for
three heartbeats.

The ritual is complete when you feel yourself return to yourself.

Chapter Seven

Firelight Bravery

The path grows darker as you walk,
not from danger,
but from the trees gathering closer
as if they want to shield you
before showing you what comes next.

Your lantern glows in your hands,
golden and steady,
casting soft circles of light
on the roots and stones beneath your boots.

Then,
up ahead,
you see it.
A faint flicker.
Not lantern-light.
Not moonlight.
Not fireflies.
Something warmer.
Something alive.

You follow the flicker
as it grows
and grows
until the path widens
into the Courage Clearing.
Above them,
small flames float in the air,

star-bright,
gentle,
moving like tiny birds
made of light.
One drifts toward you,
hovering near your shoulder
with a curious tilt,
glowing softly against your cloak.

It is warm without burning.
Brave without shouting.
Bright without blinding.
You lift your lantern,
and the floating flame moves closer
as if wanting to look inside it.

Your lantern's glow responds,
flaring just a little,
as though the firelight has encouraged it.
Encouraged you.

            You step into the clearing.
        The floating flames gather around you,
            rising and falling like breathing.
                They do not roar.
                They do not crackle.
            They burn with a quiet courage,
        the kind that doesn't try to prove anything.
            The kind that simply exists.

One flame dips low
and brushes lightly against your hand.
A warmth spreads through your fingers,
up your arm,
into your chest.
It settles there,
not like a spark,
but like the soft beginning
of a sunrise.
And suddenly you understand:

Bravery isn't loud.
It's steady.
It's the fire that warms you
before it ever tries to shine.
You sit on one of the glowing stones.
The warmth beneath you hums,
a slow, pulsing rhythm
that matches something deep inside your ribs.

You close your eyes.
The flames circle around you,
hovering at a gentle distance,
never pressing forward,
never shrinking away.

They trust you
to come closer
when you're ready.
And you do.
Not because you're fearless,
but because something inside you
no longer needs to hide from the fire.

A soft rustle of leaves
echoes above the treetops.
Then a deep, warm rumble
your dragon guardian shifting, exhaling,
settling into a place where it can watch you
without being seen.

Not guarding you from danger,
but witnessing your courage
as it grows.
You open your eyes.
Your lantern glows brighter now,
not from the flames around you,
but from the fire inside you
that you didn't know was waiting.

You stand.
The flames drift upward
in tiny arcs of gold,
as though bowing
to the bravery you found

not by fighting,
but by staying.
By being here.
By being you.
You lift your lantern one last time
toward the ring of light.
The flames flicker in reply
soft, warm, proud.

Then they rise,
floating gently into the treetops
like fireflies becoming stars.
And you step out of the Courage Clearing
with a warmth in your chest
that wasn't there before.
A fire
that doesn't roar,
but endures.

A Witchling's Flame of Courage

Sit or stand comfortably.
Feel your feet steady on the ground
like stones in the clearing.
Place your hands over your chest.
Let your palms rest gently
where your courage lives.
Take a soft, slow breath in.
Imagine a small, warm flame
glowing in your chest.

Hold for one heartbeat.
Let the warmth settle
like a quiet promise.
Exhale gently.
Feel the flame grow steadier,
not brighter,
just more yours.
Whisper softly:

"My courage is warm.
My courage is steady.
My courage belongs to me."
Stay still for a moment.
Let the warmth spread
through your shoulders,
down your arms,
into your hands.

The ritual is complete
when the warmth
feels real,
even if it is very small.

Chapter Eight

The Sunstone Path

The forest brightens as you walk,
not suddenly,
but the way morning arrives,
soft at first,
then warm enough to be felt
before you even see the light.

Your lantern glows brighter on its own,
as if it knows exactly
where you're going.
The trees thin out,
branches parting like curtains,
and you step into a narrow pathway
lined with stones that shimmer
a soft, sunrise gold.
The Sunstone Path.

Each stone gives off its own gentle warmth,
like sunlight caught in crystal
and kept safe for moments
just like this one.
You kneel to touch the nearest stone.
It is warm,
not hot,
not sharp,
just warm in a way
that feels like hands held around yours
on a cold morning.
The moment your fingers rest on it,
a small pulse of light rises through the stone,
soft and golden,
spreading into your palm.
Then you hear it,
a whisper.

Not the kind that comes from the trees
or the wind
or the creek.
This whisper comes from somewhere deeper.
Somewhere quieter.
Somewhere inside you.
It says:
"You are more than you think."
The Sunstone glows brighter.
Another whisper follows:
"Your light is older than your doubt."
The pulse settles into your hand,
steady and warm.
A gentle breeze sweeps through the path,
stirring the nearby branches.
Sunlight filters through leaves
as though the sky itself
is listening.
You stand,
your fingers still tingling from the warmth.

The stones ahead begin to glow
one by one,
as if inviting you to walk.
So you do.
Each step warms the soles of your boots,
not with heat,
but with truth.
Not loud truth.
Not truth you shout to be believed.
But the kind that rises inside you
like dawn.
The kind you can forget
when the world is too sharp,
but that never forgets you.
Halfway down the path,
you see something unexpected:
a small Sunstone shaped
like a heart.
It glows brighter than the rest
and hums softly when you lift it.

You close your fingers around it.
The warmth spreads up your arm
and into your chest,
settling in a place
that sometimes feels hollow.
You breathe in.
The stone's light brightens.
You breathe out.

The warmth deepens.
And then,
the whisper again,
this time clearer:
"You speak kinder to others
than you speak to yourself."
You swallow.

The stone waits.
Its glow does not fade.
It stays steady.
Patient.
Warm.
Another whisper follows:

Another whisper follows:
"Try speaking to yourself
the way you speak to the ones you love."
The warmth inside you widens.

Not painfully,
but tenderly,
the way a wound opens
not to hurt,
but to heal.
You lift your lantern.
Its flame shifts,
not to orange,
not to red,
but to a warm gold
that matches the stones.

It flickers as if saying:
"This light is yours.
It always was."

The forest grows quiet around you,
a quiet so deep
that you feel held by it.
Up in the treetops,
you hear the faint rustle of wings,
your dragon guardian circling slowly,
casting flashes of soft green light
between the leaves.
Not watching.
Encouraging.

You place the heart-shaped Sunstone
into your pocket.
It glows through the fabric,
warming your side
like a small positive thought
you can keep close.
The Sunstone Path leads you onward,
its light steady,
its warmth patient.
And with each step,
you begin to learn:

The words you say to yourself
can shape the world you walk in.
The path ends,
but the warmth doesn't.
It settles in your lantern.
It settles in your chest.
It settles in your steps
as you continue deeper into the Woods.

A Witchling's Light of Kindness

Hold your hands together
as if cupping a small glowing stone.
Close your eyes.
Imagine a warm golden light
resting between your palms.
Breathe in slowly.

Let the light grow brighter.
Breathe out softly.
Let the light settle into your chest.

The ritual is complete
when the light feels like
something
you deserve to keep.

Whisper:
"My light is gentle.
My light is real.
My light belongs to me."
Think of one kind sentence
you would say to someone you love.
Speak it silently
to yourself.
Hold the warmth for three breaths.

Chapter Nine

The

Moonmirror Pond

The forest grows quieter as you follow
the Sunstone Path,
its golden glow fading gently behind you
like the last warm breath of afternoon.
The trees begin to thin,
their branches arching overhead
in soft silver curves.
The air cools.
The light softens.
And you feel it before you see it,
a pull,
a hush,
a stillness
waiting just ahead.
You step into a wide clearing
where the sky opens above you
like a held breath released.
In the center of the clearing
rests a perfect round pond.
Still.
Dark.
Shining.

The Moonmirror Pond.
Its surface is so smooth
that it looks like a piece of the night sky
fell into the forest and stayed.
No ripples.
No movement.
Just quiet, shimmering truth.
Your lantern's glow dances across the water,
and the reflection forms two lights,
one above,
one below.
You kneel at the edge.
The pond reflects you
not as you appear,
but as you feel.
And tonight...
you feel like someone
carrying more than you ever say aloud.

The water brightens
just slightly
beneath your gaze.
Not in judgment.
In recognition.
A firefly drifts low above the Pond,
its glow doubling across the surface
like twin stars moving together.
You reach your hand toward the water
but stop just above the surface.
Something tells you
the pond will speak
only if you are very, very gentle.
A breeze moves across the clearing,
but the water does not ripple.
Only when you breathe out
do the tiniest circles form,
slow, widening rings of silver light.

A whisper rises from the pond.
Not in words.
Not in sound.
In knowing.
A knowing that feels like:
"You already have the answers
you keep asking for."
You touch the water with one fingertip.
The surface lights up,
a soft glow spreading outward
like moonlight sliding across glass.
For a moment,
you see not your face,
but your self:
Your hurts.
Your hopes.
Your hidden strength.
Your quieter thoughts
that you don't always trust
but that have never been wrong.

You lift your lantern a little higher.
The flame reflects in the Pond
as a long golden ribbon—
a path of light
stretching into the center of the still water.
You follow the reflection with your eyes.
It leads you to a single lily pad
floating alone in the middle of the Pond.
On it rests a crystal.
Small.
Silver.
Softly glowing.
A Moonstone.
It glimmers
like a thought you haven't said aloud yet.
You hold your breath.
The pond waits.
The Moonstone pulses once,
as if answering a question
you didn't realize you were asking.
And then you understand:
Reflection doesn't always mean looking back.

Sometimes it means looking inward.
You dip your hand into the Pond.
The water is cool,
but not cold.
Refreshing.
Clarifying.
Revealing.
The surface steadies again
as you withdraw your hand.
A ripple runs outward
and the Moonstone brightens
as if saying,
"Yes. You're listening."
A shadow circles above,
large wings brushing moonlight aside.
Your dragon guardian glides silently overhead,
casting silver shapes across the clearing
before settling somewhere in the dark pines
with a low, approving rumble.
The glow spreads across the water
in a wide, quiet wave,
so soft
you can barely see it.

Its presence feels like reassurance,
as though it trusts your inner knowing
even when you don't.
You sit a moment longer,
your lantern resting beside you,
your reflection shimmering like a promise.
When you stand,
the Pond glows softly behind you,
as if holding a memory:
A quiet version of you
who listens to their own truth
even when the world is too loud.
You take one last look
at the Moonmirror Pond.
Its surface shines
not with answers,
but with clarity.
You lift your lantern.
And the forest path ahead
lights up
as if your intuition
has already chosen the way.

A Witchling's Whisper of Knowing

Sit quietly.
Let your hands rest in your lap
like calm water.
Imagine a still pond
reflecting moonlight.
Place one hand over your chest.
Feel the slow rise and fall
like gentle ripples.
Breathe in softly.
Let the breath feel smooth,
steady,
unforced.
Breathe out gently.
Imagine a ripple moving outward
from the center of the pond.

Whisper:
"I listen to the quiet place inside me."
Think of one question
you carry within you.
Hold it lightly.
Don't force the answer.
Let it drift to the surface
on its own time.
Rest for three breaths.

The ritual is complete
when the light feels
like something
you deserve to keep.

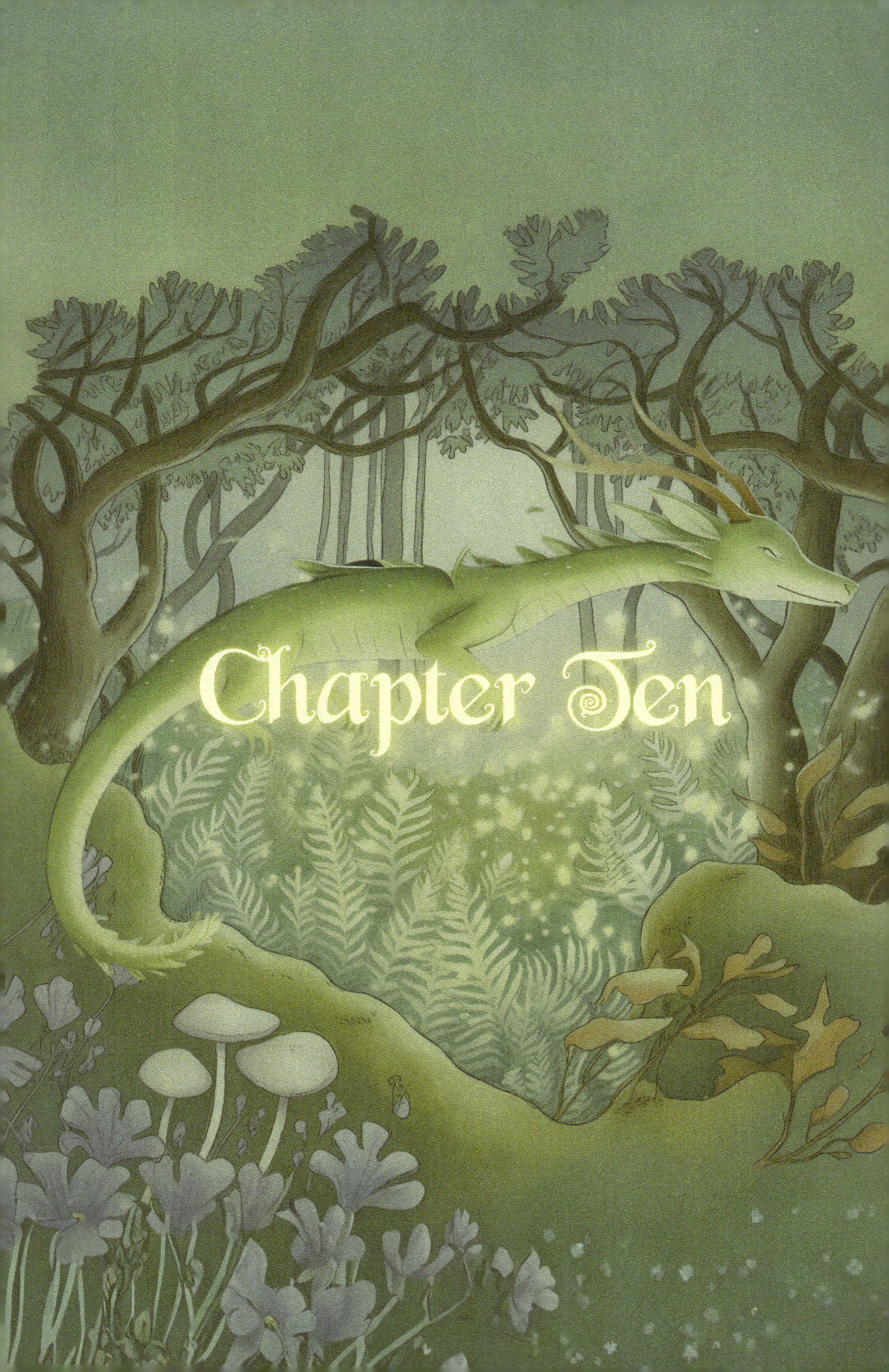
Chapter Ten

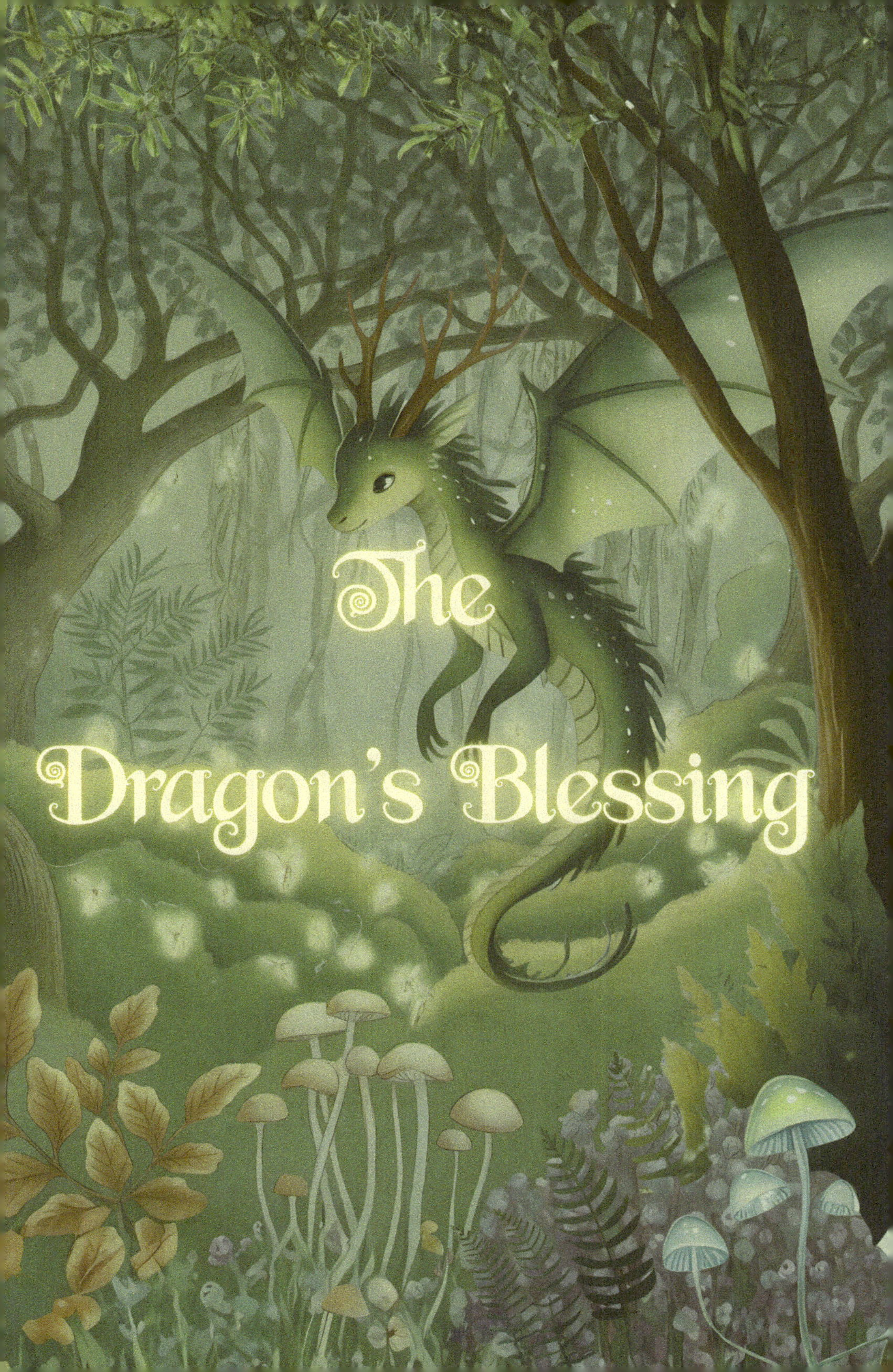
The
Dragon's Blessing

The night deepens as you walk,
but the darkness doesn't frighten you anymore.
It feels soft
and full
and alive
in the same way the sky feels alive
when it carries more stars
than your eyes can count.

Your lantern glows steadily at your side,
not brighter than before,
but truer.
Its light feels like something
that has grown with you
instead of ahead of you.
The trees stretch taller,
their branches arching like cathedral ceilings
woven from silver leaves and moon-soaked bark

A warmth settles in your chest
not firelight,
not sunlight,
but something in between

Something that feels like you.
Then you hear it.
A low, deep rumble
rolling across the treetops.
Not thunder.
Not wind.
Not danger.
Recognition.
You step into a wide clearing lit only by moonlight.
The trees fall back,
forming a half-circle around a smooth stone
as tall as your waist
and warm with ancient magic.
You place your lantern on it.
The flame steadies.
The air thickens.
The clearing breathes.
And then the shadows shift.
A long shape unfurls between the trees
soft as smoke,
quiet as breath.

Your dragon guardian emerges
from the forest's deepest dark.
Not with fangs.
Not with fire.
Not with fear.
With grace.
Its moss-green scales shimmer
like leaves dipped in moonlight.
Its antlers rise like branches,
carved by centuries of wind.
Its eyes glow warm gold,
soft enough to rest in,
deep enough to feel seen.
The dragon lowers its great head
until its nose rests just inches from you.
You do not move.
Not because you are frozen
but because you are home.
The dragon inhales slowly,
a breath that pulls the mist toward it,
carrying the scents of pine,
lantern smoke,
and your courage.

On the exhale,
a soft warm breeze rolls over you.
Not hot.
Not startling.
Just warm enough
to settle something inside you
that has been restless for a very long time.
You place your hand on the dragon's snout.
The dragon closes its eyes.
Light blooms beneath your palm,
gold, then green,
then soft white
like a star being born
at the edge of your fingers.
A hum vibrates through the clearing,
through the trees,
through your arm,
through your lantern.
A heartbeat.
Your heartbeat.
The dragon's heartbeat.
The forest's heartbeat.
All recognizing one another.

All recognizing one another.
All agreeing on something quietly:
You are stronger now.
Not because you found magic,
but because you found your own.
The dragon only reflected what was
already inside you.
The dragon lifts its head
and looks at you with an ancient, steady softness.
Then it bows.
A creature older than storms,
older than mountains,
bows to you.
Not because you are powerful
in the way stories often claim power looks.
But because you are powerful
in the way truth looks.
Quiet.
Steady.
Courageous
in the gentlest way.

The dragon steps back into the shadows,
scales blending with leaves,
eyes lingering like warm lanterns in the night.
When its shape disappears completely,
you feel it,
not leaving you,
but becoming part of the Woods around you.
Part of the path.
Part of the breath.
Part of the knowing.
You lift your lantern.
Its flame is steady.
Warm.
And yours.
You walk toward the trees ahead,
and the forest parts for you
like it always meant to,

because you are not just a visitor anymore.
You are a Witchling of the Woods
with a dragon's blessing
resting quietly in your chest.
And wherever you go next,
in the Woods
or in the world,
your light walks with you.

A Witchling's Spell of Self-Trust

Place your hands together
as if holding something
warm and alive.
Close your eyes.
Imagine a long dragon shape
curled protectively around
your heart.

Breathe in slowly.
Feel the dragon's warmth
rise inside your chest.
Breathe out gently.

Let the warmth settle deeper.
Whisper softly:
"I trust the quiet magic in me.
I trust the truth I carry.
I trust my own light.

Lift your chin slightly,
as if receiving a dragon's nod.
Hold the warmth for three
breaths.

**The ritual is complete
when you feel steadier
than you did before.**

Chapter Eleven

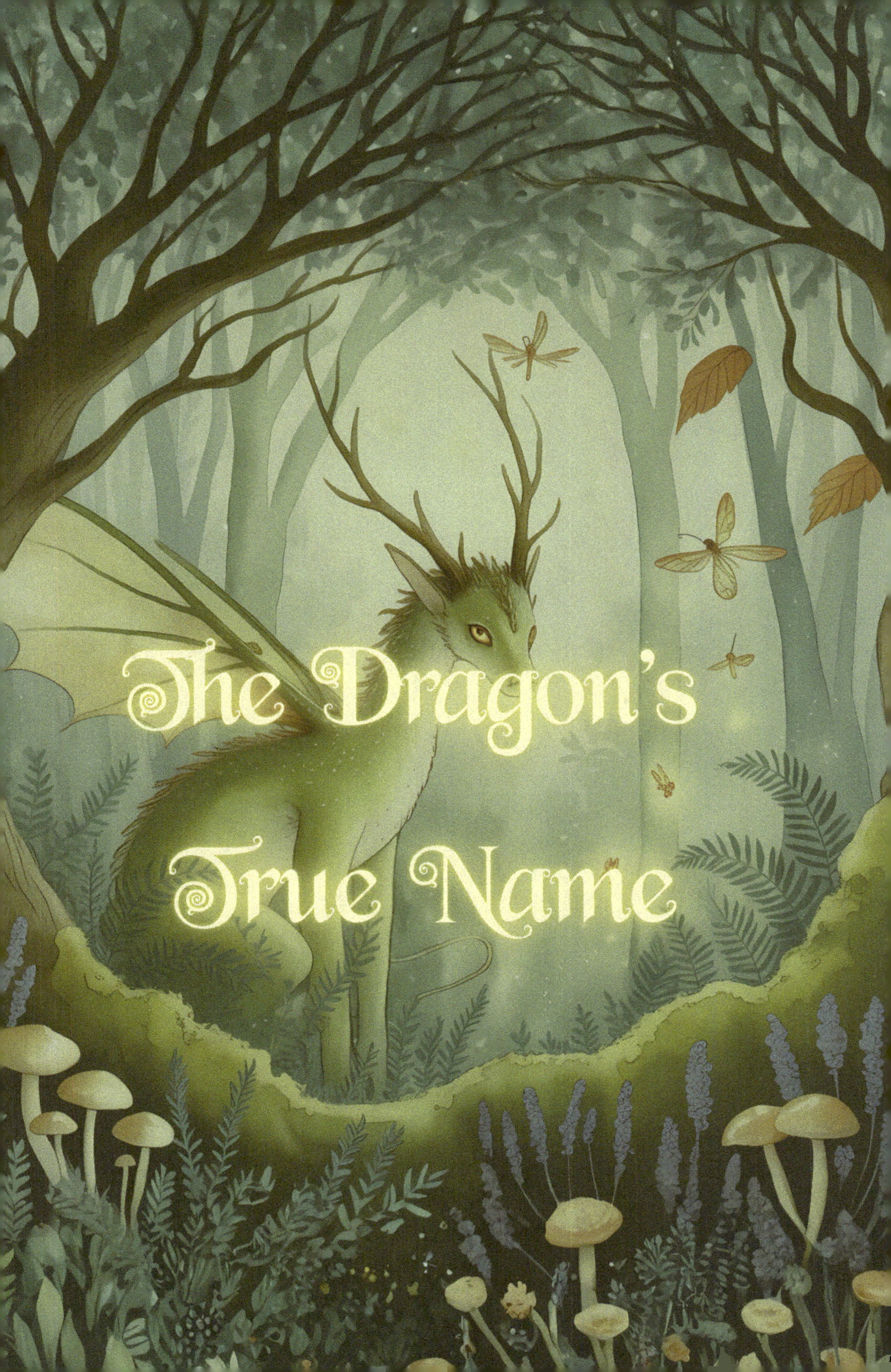
The Dragon's
True Name

The moon is high
when you feel the tug in your chest
a soft, familiar pull
that feels like the forest
calling you back for one last secret.
You follow the pull
to a narrow path
lit only by your own steps.
And then you see it:
A clearing
you've never visited before.
Not grand.
Not glowing.
Just quiet.

In the center lies a pool of starlight
still as glass.
Your dragon guardian rises from the shadows,
soft and enormous,
eyes glowing with a warmth
you know anywhere.
It lowers its head
and breathes a ribbon of silver light
across the starlit pool.
The surface ripples—
not outward,
but inward,
toward a single point of soft glow.
A whisper forms in your mind.

A name.
Not in words.
In feeling.
It feels like:
Warmth.
Truth.
Courage.
Home.
You.
Because the dragon's true name
is not something separate from you.
It is the part of you
that stayed soft
when the world felt sharp.

The part that kept glowing
when you felt dim.
The part that trusted you
long before you trusted yourself.
The name rises in your chest
like a lantern lit from within.
You place your hand over your heart.
And the dragon bows—
a bow not of ownership,
but of recognition.
Because now you finally know:
The dragon's true name
is the same name
as your quiet strength.
And it has always
belonged
to you.

Dear Little

Witchling

Dear Little Witchling,

You've walked the forest paths with such courage,
even on the pages where you weren't
sure you had any.
You've breathed with the wind,
stood steady with the roots,
listened to the water,
and felt firelight warm your chest
in the gentlest way.
And step by step,
spell by soft spell,
you discovered something important:
The magic was never in the Woods.

It was in you the whole time.
The lantern you carry now
doesn't glow because of this book,
or the dragon,
or the rituals.
It glows because of your bravery,
your kindness,
your questions,
and the quiet strength
you let yourself feel.

You are a Witchling of the Woods now,
not because you finished reading,
but because you learned to trust
your own light.
Wherever you go next,
the Woods walk with you.
Your dragon watches from the sky.
And your magic stays steady in your chest.
You are ready for whatever comes next.
And your lantern
will never go out.

The Witchling's

Path Beyond

the Woods

The forest stands behind you now,
but its warmth hums quietly
in the center of your chest
like a lantern you no longer need to hold
to feel its glow.
The Heartstone in your pocket
presses gently against your side.
The Sunstone's warmth lingers in your palms.
Your breath moves the way wind moves—
soft, steady, knowing.
And your dragon...
You can't see them,
but you feel the shadow of their wings

somewhere above you,
a familiar comfort
like a hand resting lightly
between your shoulder blades.
You step beyond the last tree,
and the world opens.
Not a forest.
Not a path.
Not a place with rules or rituals.
Just life
stretching wide in every direction.
You do not know what waits for you next.
But you know something far more important:
You are ready for it.
Because courage is not loud.
Calm is not stillness.

Magic is not something you learn,
it is something you remember.
You walk forward, lantern-light in your chest,
and the forest behind you glows softly
for a moment
long enough to whisper:
"Once a Witchling of the Woods,
always a Witchling of the Woods."
And wherever you go,
the path will know your footsteps.
And the dragon
will know your name.

Closing Ritual

The Lantern-Home Spell
Sit or stand comfortably.
Feel the way your body rests,
steady like roots,
warm like sunshine.
Close your eyes gently.
Remember the forest paths,
the lanterns,
the dragon's wings over you.
Place one hand over your heart.
Feel the beat,
feel the glow,
like a small warm light inside.
Take a slow breath in.
The Woods breathe with you.
Exhale softly.

The lantern inside you glows.
Whisper, slowly — like a soft spell:
"The Woods walk with me.
My lantern stays lit.
The magic is mine."
Open your eyes.
Notice how the world feels now,
a little softer,
a little safer,
a little more yours.

The ritual is complete
when you feel even a small warmth in your chest,
a glow you can take with you
wherever you go.
Because the magic was never something you found.
It was something you remembered.

Dear Witchling,

If you are reading these words,
know this first:
You are not alone.
Not in your fear,
not in your questions,
not in your quiet feelings
that sometimes feel too big.
There is a kind of magic
that grows in gentle hearts,
a magic that does not spark or roar,
but hums like lantern-light
in the quiet places of your chest.

That magic lives in you.
This book was written
to help you hear it.
Every spell is a breath.
Every ritual is a moment.
Every clearing teaches you something
you already carry
but may have forgotten.
The Woods will walk with you
as long as you need them.
And when you step beyond these pages,
the magic will come with you.
I am so proud of your courage.
Keep your lantern close
and your feet soft on the path.

With warmth always,
Wilhelmina Woods

A Note for Parents, Caregivers & Wellness Guides

Dear Grown-Up,
Thank you for placing this book in a young person's hands.
The Little Witch of the Woods was created as
a soft landing place,
a book to help children feel steadier inside themselves,
especially on the days when emotions run high,
worries feel heavy,
or the world seems too loud.
Within these pages, children will learn:

- how to calm their breath
- how to feel grounded and safe in their body
- how to move through big emotions gently
- how to speak kindly to themselves
- how to find courage without pressure or force
- how to trust their inner wisdom

This is not instruction in supernatural magic
or occult practice.
The "spells" and "rituals" within the book are metaphors,
gentle mindfulness tools disguised in wonder
to make emotional skills approachable, memorable, and safe.

Every ritual is based in evidence-backed calming strategies:
- deep breathing
- visualization
- grounding
- emotional reflection
- self-affirmation

The Woods give children a safe place to explore
their thoughts, their feelings, and their inner strength
in a way that feels playful, imaginative, and non-threatening.
You may wish to read alongside your child,
or you may let them wander through the Forest
at their own pace.
Some children will absorb the magic silently,
while others may open to you through conversation.
Both ways are perfect.
If you'd like to support them further, you might ask:
- "Which part of the Woods did you visit today?"
- "What did your lantern feel like?"
- "Did a ritual help you breathe easier?"
- "What magic did you discover inside yourself?"

There are no tests, no expectations, no right answers.
This book is not here to measure your child ,
it is here to meet them.
Thank you for trusting this journey.
Thank you for holding space for slow-growing courage.
Thank you for being part of the Woods with us.
With warmth and wonder,
Wilhelmina Woods

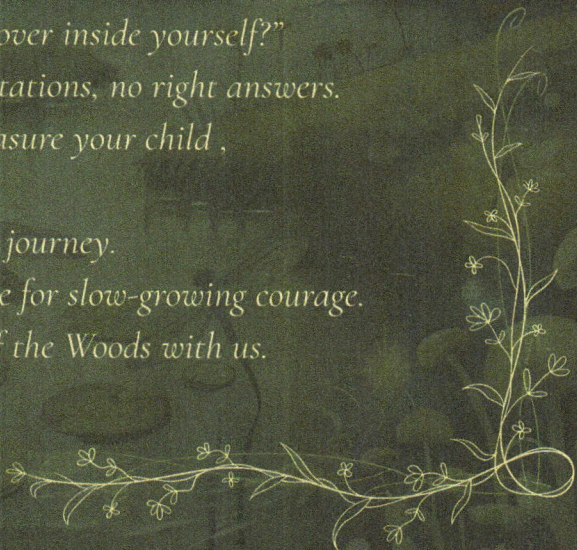

This book can support emotional regulation work in counselling rooms, classrooms, and therapeutic environments.
Each chapter contains metaphor-based emotional learning:

CHAPTERSKILL

The Forest Door	**Regulation + readiness**
The Lantern Pathway	**Anxiety calming + step-thinking**
The Root Rise	**Grounding + safety in the body**
The Whispering Grove	**Breathwork + mindfulness awareness**
The Water Whispers	**Emotional flow + processing feelings**
The Circle Grove	**Gentle boundary-setting**
Firelight Bravery	**Courage building without pressure**
The Sunstone Path	**Self-kindness + inner worth**
The Moonmirror Pond	**Intuition + reflection**
The Dragon's Blessing	**Self-trust + internal support**

Use as:

➤ *A weekly emotional learning tool*
➤ *Guided reading during therapy sessions*
➤ *Calming support for neurodivergent youth*
➤ *A resource for anxiety, sensory overwhelm, grief + identity work*

This book is trauma-safe, shame-free, and written to protect tender nervous systems.
It meets children where they are — softly, respectfully, never forcefully.
Invite journaling, breath exercises, or quiet listening to deepen the work.
The magic is metaphor — the healing is real.

Discussion Guide

For Grown-Ups

&

Little Witchlings

Use these prompts gently — not as quizzes — but as lanterns for conversation.
After reading a chapter, you might ask:

🌿 *What part of the Woods did you walk through today?*
🌿 *Which ritual helped*

These questions are meant to open gentle dialogue —
not to test understanding, but to build connection.
Use one or two at a time, never all at once.
Let the child lead where the conversation goes.

AFTER ANY CHAPTER

🌿 *Which part of the Woods did you visit today?*
🌿 *What did it feel like inside your chest while you were reading?*
🌿 *Did anything in the story remind you of yourself?*

ABOUT THE RITUALS

🌿 *Which ritual felt easiest? Which one felt harder? Why?*
🌿 *Did you feel anything change in your body or breath?*
🌿 *Would you like to try one together?*

CONNECTION & FEELINGS

- *Is there a chapter you want to go back to when you're upset or worried?*
- *What does "calm" feel like to you? What does "courage" feel like?*
- *Did the Woods teach you something new today?*

SELF-BELIEF & CONFIDENCE

- *What did your lantern light show you about yourself?*
- *Where do you feel strongest or bravest inside you?*
- *What magic inside you felt brightest today?*

WHEN A CHILD FEELS STUCK

- *If the Witchling were here, what might they tell you?*
- *Would your dragon have a message for you right now?*
- *If we walked through the forest together, where would we go?*

These questions are meant to spark reflection, not pressure. Soft is enough. Short is enough. Silence is sometimes an answer too.

Daily Practice Page

A Gentle Witchling Routine

No timers.
No perfect days.
Just small moments of magic.
You may print this, journal with it, or whisper it to yourself
before bed.

🌿 1. Read a Lantern Page

Just one chapter, or even one paragraph.
Let the Woods speak softly.

🌿 2. Light-Heart Breath (30 seconds)

Breathe in like a lantern warming,
breathe out like its glow spreading.

🌿 3. Choose One Feeling to Hold Today

Examples:

🌿 calm
🌿 brave
🌿 steady
🌿 gentle
🌿 kind to myself

Write or whisper:

"Today, my magic feels ___."

4. A Witchling Reflection

Pick one:

- A moment I was brave
- A moment I felt unsure (that's okay)
- A ritual I want to try again

You may write, draw, or just think it.

5. Carry One Lantern Thought

Choose a sentence like a pocket-stone:

- My courage is quiet and real.
- I listen to the gentle truth inside me.
- I take one small step at a time.
- My roots hold me when things feel big.

Say it once in the morning.
Once in the evening.
That's enough.

The Practice is Complete When...

Your chest feels softer,
your breath feels steadier,
or your light feels just a little more your own.
Even a tiny glow counts as magic.

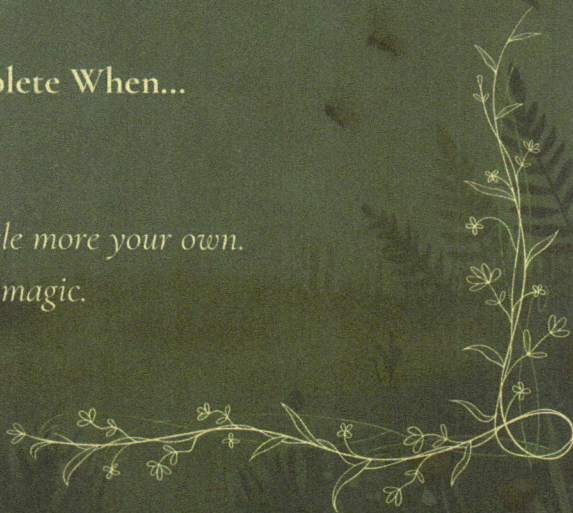

Glossary

Of Magical

Elements

Lantern-Light
The warm glow inside you that helps you feel safe, calm, and steady. Your inner compass.

Heartstone
A symbol of your inner courage and emotional truth. A reminder that your feelings matter.

Sunstone
A warm golden stone that represents self-kindness and positive self-talk.

Moonstone
A soft silver stone that represents intuition, clarity, and quiet knowing.

Root Magic
Grounding energy that helps you feel stable, supported, and protected.

Wind Spells
Breathwork disguised as forest magic. Helps you release tension and settle your thoughts.

Water Whispers

Emotional flow. The reminder that feelings can move
through you gently and safely.

Circle Magic

Boundaries. Knowing where you begin and where the world ends.

Firelight Bravery

The quiet courage that burns inside you,
even when you feel small.

Moonmirror Pond

Reflection and self-awareness. Seeing yourself honestly,
kindly, and clearly.

Dragon Guardian

Your self-trust. The quiet part of you that knows your worth even
when you forget.

The Woods

A safe, magical space inside you where your feelings can rest
and your courage can grow.

www.ingramcontent.com/pod-product-compliance
Lightning Source LLC
Chambersburg PA
CBHW060403090426
42734CB00011B/2251